RAILS ACROSS NORTH AMERICA

A PICTORIAL JOURNEY ACROSS THE USA

RAILS ACROSS NORTH AMERICA

A PICTORIAL JOURNEY ACROSS THE USA

DAVID CABLE

PEN & SWORD
TRANSPORT

First published in Great Britain in 2015 by
Pen & Sword Transport
An imprint of Pen & Sword Books Ltd
47 Church Street
Barnsley
South Yorkshire
S70 2AS

ISBN 9781473838055

Printed and bound by Imago Publishing Limited.

Pen & Sword Books Ltd incorporates the imprints of Pen & Sword Archaeology, Atlas, Aviation, Battleground, Discovery, Family History, History, Maritime, Military, Naval, Politics, Railways, Select, Social History, Transport, True Crime, and Claymore Press, Frontline Books, Leo Cooper, Praetorian Press, Remember When, Seaforth Publishing and Wharncliffe.

For a complete list of Pen and Sword titles please contact
Pen and Sword Books Limited
47 Church Street, Barnsley, South Yorkshire, S70 2AS, England
E-mail: enquiries@pen-and-sword.co.uk
Website: www.pen-and-sword.co.uk

DAVID CABLE – OTHER PUBLICATIONS

Railfreight in Colour (for the modeller and historian)

BR Passenger Sectors in Colour (for the modeller and historian)

Lost Liveries of Privatisation in Colour (for the modeller and historian)

Hydraulics in the West

The Blue Diesel Era

Introduction

Between 1966 and 2008, I have had the opportunity to visit the USA on seventeen occasions, four of which were combined with visits to Canada (which are the subject of another book). In total I have photographed trains in thirty-nine states.

The first three trips were for business purposes, those from 1991 to 1999 with my wife, Glenda, and those subsequent either on my own or meeting up with a group of American train enthusiasts, a nice group of about fifty members calling themselves the WGRF – the World's Greatest Rail Fans, although a number of people in the UK, Germany, Switzerland and Australia to name but a few would dispute that title!

The 1966 trip was an exception. I was due to fly back from Australia to England, following a two month project, and at the last minute was asked to spend a week with an associate company in Columbus OH. My plans to sightsee in New York City on the Saturday afternoon before my flight home, were scuppered when I became stranded in Pittsburgh Airport, due to the east coast being fog bound, no flights being able to get there. So I had recourse to going via the Pennsylvania Railroad in a train comprising three E8A locos, nineteen baggage cars and two passenger cars tacked on the back. I recall going round Horseshoe Curve looking across at the locos. But on this trip I had no camera with me.

All the other sixteen trips provided opportunities for me to photograph the American railroad scene, and this book contains a selection of what I saw.

The book is arranged in date sequence, and in the order of the visits made to the different locations in the course of each trip.

The first trip in 1975 was undertaken as a site selection visit for a major British company, a spectacularly exhausting trip with little opportunity to take photos, but my colleague and I, who had visited different states independently, met up in Washington DC one weekend, and our sightseeing encompassed the Union station. Later on, we both stayed in Asheville NC, where the loco shed was visited.

The 1986 trip was taken with three colleagues from Blue Circle Cement, when we visited the four US cement works owned by the company in Georgia, Alabama, Oklahoma and New York states, which did provide for some pictures to be taken. One of the Blue Circle management also arranged for me to go round the loco shed at Selkirk NY, and also spend some time in the control tower for the hump yard – quite an experience!

From 1991 to 1999, with one exception in 1997, all the trips were undertaken with Glenda. She was a very skilled patchwork/quilting exponent, and seized the chance to visit various centres and meeting groups associated with this hobby, as well as purchasing large quantities of materials! The trips were planned by examining catalogues, which showed where interesting events, which she would like to attend, were to be held and when. I would then check if there were any railroad locations fairly close by, and from that our itinerary, sometimes quite circuitous, was developed. So while she met up with her associates, I went off trackside, although there were quite a number of days when we shared our hobbies – I would carry all the material and books she bought, and she would sit by the tracks sewing, and when a train came past, would take the numbers of the second, fourth , sixth etc. locos!

In 1991, we flew to Vancouver BC to stay with Glenda's family, and with them did a round trip, staying initially in Vancouver WA, where we had a hotel room overlooking the Burlington Northern line east. I hired a taxi and said to the driver 'Take me to the engine sheds', whereupon he took me to both the Southern Pacific and Union Pacific facilities in Portland OR, and waited while I took my shots, quite astonished at my hobby!

The 1993 trip started by flying to Chicago and staying in Aurora IL, which involved shopping in Chicago, but also visits to West Chicago and Eola yard, which was accessible at both ends in those days. From there we travelled to Paducah KY, the headquarters of the American Quilting Society, but also the workshops of VMV in the old Illinois Central buildings! From there we went to Denver, including Palmer Lake, and a solo trip to Cheyenne. Quilting in Lancaster CA was next on the list, which also gave the means to go to Cajon Summit and Tehachapi for the loop. We then flew back to stay in Brunswick, MD, where I covered lines between Washington DC and Baltimore and various other locations.

We started off in 1994 at Providence RI. Various short lines in the area plus Boston commuter services provided a springboard to go across to the Hudson valley at Peekskill followed by Binghamton. Travelling on to near Lake Erie, the old main Pennsylvania line was photographed near Harrisburg amongst other locations. Our final US destination was outside Buffalo, where a wealth of photos was obtained in this busy railroad area. The trip concluded in Canada via Niagara Falls.

In 1995, my wife had booked to go to a conference in Houston in November, so we thought we would start off in Arizona, first in Tucson and then Flagstaff. In perfect weather, I got many shots on the SP Sunset route and the ATSF main line from Chicago to California, plus some nice short lines. A trip into Mexico was also undertaken. Arizona gave us the chance to do some sightseeing, which is something we always tried to fit in. In Texas, the weather had gone downhill, and I spent my days either trying to keep warm or dry, taking pictures in far from ideal lighting conditions.

The year 1997 started again by flying to Chicago, this time staying in Rockford IL. Whilst Glenda did her own things, I started off at Rochelle, standing in the middle of the UP and BN crossing, as happy as a sand boy with all the traffic. We visited a couple of locations in Wisconsin, before going to Grand Island NE, Minneapolis for the Mall of America (yuk!), Rapid City SD, the Alliance loco shed of BNSF, and on to Denver again from where we flew home.

In the second part of 1997, I was invited, quite out of the blue, to stay with a person from whom I had purchased some slides, Bob Graham and his wife Parker, who lived in Reidsville NC. Bob was at work during the week, so I made my own way around with his advice, but at the weekend he made sure I was properly taken around. Bob was the person who introduced me to the WGRF later on. I carried on afterwards into South Carolina and Georgia, where I saw a lot of short lines to add to the collection.

The first 1999 trip to the US with Glenda started in Pennsylvania, where she wanted to visit a huge patchwork shop at Intercourse (when we returned she told the ladies at the Women's Institute, where she had been, having phrased it to perfection; a gasp echoed round the hall). From there we made our way back again to Paducah and another visit round the workshops, and returned to Rockford IL again, which gave me a chance to do more in Wisconsin and the main lines west from Chicago.

My final trip with her followed another visit to her family in Canada, from where we flew to Calgary so as to get to Glacier Park MT and Helena, where we had an idyllic time enjoying the trains and the scenery.

After my wife died in early 2001, I made a trip round the world, visiting family, and friends, and spent a few days on the west coast, but later that year undertook my first trip with the WGRF, with whom I felt most welcome. The WGRF have a volunteer each year, who organizes visits in his own area particularly to short lines and industrial locations, which are not normally accessible to the public, and often contain locos out of the ordinary. The 2001 meeting was based in Kansas City, which I followed by visiting California on my own. On the day I was due to fly back to New York and the UK, some unmentionables (I am being politically correct, which goes against the grain!) blew up the Trade Centre in NYC. I was therefore stranded for a week in Tehachapi, where the famous loop is, and fortunately had enough film with me to last the time!

In 2002, another WGRF member, Roger Bee, invited me to stay with him and his wife Rita, at their home at Corinth near Fort Worth TX. Apart from many local visits, we also made a large circular trip through Louisiana, Mississippi, a corner of Alabama, Arkansas and Oklahoma. I finished up for a few days in the New York City area.

The WGRF meetings in 2003, 2004 and 2005 were based in Indianapolis, St Louis and Akron OH respectively, although I visited the New England states before the 2003 get-together. The final trip I made was to the 2008 WGRF meeting based at Aberdeen NC, and I rounded off the trip seeing trains on the two major lines in Nebraska.

In the text of the captions, there are various abbreviations and locomotive classifications. The locomotive classifications can be summarized as;

GP (General Purpose 4 axle), SD (Special Duty six axle), SW and MP (4 axle switchers) are designs manufactured by Electro Motive Division, formerly part of General Motors. The higher the number, the higher the horsepower, but if multiplied by 100 does not reflect the actual power. B, C, U and ES prefixes to a number denote locos built by General Electric.

As an example C44-9W represents a six axle, 4400 HP loco with category 9 electronic controls and a full-width cab.

So what has happened during the bulk of my visits?

First has been the consolidation of the four major class 1 railroads through mergers and acquisitions. Burlington Northern (BN) and Atchison, Topeka & Santa Fe (ATSF) merged to become Burlington Northern Santa Fe (BNSF); CSX Transportation (CSX) took over half of Conrail (CR) which was no longer viable as an independent organization; Norfolk Southern (NS) took over the rest of Conrail; and Union Pacific (UP) acquired Chicago North Western (CNW) and Denver & Rio Grande, which had in turn acquired Southern Pacific (SP). The other class 1 line, Kansas City Southern (KCS) had taken over two smaller lines.

These class 1 lines then cast off the less/un-remunerative branch lines, which has resulted in them becoming companies operating heavy, long distance trains, predominantly intermodal and coal, over long distances, using the latest third generation, high horsepower locomotives in multiple, on well maintained, heavy ballasted tracks. They have become major conglomerates and major players on the US stock markets.

Secondly, the class 2 railroads comprise a mixture of regional and short lines, with some quite lengthy routes, generally the cast offs of the class 1 lines. Canadian National has made some infiltration into the USA, with its purchasing of, originally, Grand Trunk Western and Central Vermont RRs, but more recently, Wisconsin Central and Illinois Central, giving access from Canada to the Gulf of Mexico. Canadian Pacific took over SOO line and Delaware & Hudson giving it access to Chicago and the New York to Washington DC part of the country. Several of the short lines have co-operated to form a corporate umbrella, whilst still presenting their own image, which results in interesting movements of motive power within the grouping. For example, I have seen Indiana Southern locos in Georgia and Central Oregon & Pacific locos in Texas, which makes the hobby more enjoyable.

Many other short lines are either owned by industrial companies or privately owned, using second-generation locomotives previously used by the class 1 roads until superseded by newer, more efficient, higher power designs. Most of these lines are profitable enterprises. But in some other cases, financial problems cause maintenance to be deferred, particularly of track, which results in them having severe speed restrictions, even as low as 10mph, with old rolling stock, which hardly helps them to improve. These are the class 3 lines.

Passenger services have remained fairly consistent. Amtrak still struggles to maintain an interstate service, apart from the North East Corridor, but the commuter services in some of the major cities are buoyant and well used.

So, in this book which is planned to reach rail enthusiasts, modellers and the general public, both in North America and elsewhere, I have tried to achieve a representative selection of pictures from my fairly extensive collection of what has been happening during the time of most of my visits to the USA, particularly showing a range of short lines. Whilst most pictures are of trains in action, a number have been chosen to help modellers. And being British has quite often helped to gain access to some normally unauthorised locations!

To conceive a book such as this, and to go through all my photos, has brought back many happy memories, and is a labour of love. I can only hope the pictures are of enough interest for me to be able to say 'Enjoy!'.

David Cable
Hartley Wintney, UK
September 2014

Some of the major Union stations use their own switchers for transferring or disposing of stock. In this example, Washington Terminal Alco RS1 44 is seen with some Amtrak coaches at Washington Union station. June 1975.

An Amtrak Metroliner electric multiple unit is prepared for another run up the North East Corridor from Washington Union station.

Chessie System GP40-2 4198 & 420x pass Ivy City yards outside Washington DC with a manifest freight train in June 1975.

Penn Central RS3 in 9954 sits in a field with a train of gondolas near Norfolk, VA. An unidentified switcher is at the other end of the train.

Southern GP35 213, GP30 253x, 2627 & 2618 sit on Asheville NC loco shed in July 1975.

My colleagues very kindly stopped the car on a main road over-bridge in Tulsa OK so that I could take this shot of BN switchers SW1500 61 & 300 propelling a long rake of cabooses and freight cars in the old Frisco yard. Taken in September 1986.

The size of an American freight yard is amply demonstrated by this photo taken from the control tower at Selkirk yard, NY in September 1986. Conrail MT6 slug 1112 and SD38 6947 have just finished propelling a load of cars over the hump, and are now returning for their next push.

Having been allowed access to the control tower at Selkirk I photographed CR GP38-2 8261, GP40 3213 & GP40-2 3360 turning on the shed triangle.

On the way back from Selkirk, I was fortunate enough to find two New York Central preserved locos stabled outside a power station near Ravenna NY. In front was the original NYC electric loco from 1906, S1 100 accompanied by lightning striped T3 278.

In September 1991, I called in at Cascade Locks OR, where Amtrak F40PH 300 was in charge of the eastbound 'Pioneer' section from Portland.

Plenty of colours under the sun at Brooklyn yard, Portland OR, where an exhibition had been held, including UP C40-8W 9392, SP GP60 9753 and BN GP38 2075, the Pacific Pride loco carrying the emblems of the companies that had merged to become Burlington Northern. September 1991.

Tucked behind these three locos was a nice surprise - UP SD40-2 3593 which was in camouflage commemorating the UP employees serving in the US armed forces in the Iraq campaign Desert Storm.

Washington Central GP9 301 heads GP7 4491, CF7 402 & GP7 4492 at Yakima WA in September 1991. The two GP7s have been purchased from CNW and are still in that company's colours.

An eastbound manifest freight is about to cross the EJE line at West Chicago in May 1993. The train is headed by CNW SD50 7033, UP SD40-2 3314, UP SD40-2r B3455 and CNW SD40-2 6836.

BN SD40-2 8159 & 7056 are about to enter the west end of Eola yard, IL with an eastbound manifest freight.

The full effect of the Chicago skyline in May 1993 with the Sears Tower dominant, overpowers the railroads, where an Amtrak F40PH has left Union station.

Withdrawn but still worthy of a photo, BN E9As 9910 & 9903 have finished their days running services between Chicago and Aurora IL. They are parked close to the Roosevelt Road Bridge in Chicago.

Not many photos appear of the Chicago 'EL', but here we see CTA car 2530 trailing a train which has just left Randolph & Water Street station and rounding one of the very sharp bends which characterise the system.

Absolutely ex works and restored, UP E9A 949 gleams outside the shops at VMV in May 1993. The works are at Paducah KY, and I was taken round by the Chief Executive himself - being British helps!

Four IC GP40s switch the fairly full yard at Fulton KY. In sequence they are 3109, 3117, 3108 and 3114.

A Cairo IL to Fulton KY local trip working approaches its destination behind IC GP10 8109. Near the rear of the train is what purports to be the Amtrak station, served by a train during the night. As you can see, very hospitable for travellers!

Rio Grande line up at Denver North yard. On the left GP30 3018, in the centre SW1000 146 and on the right
GP60 3156. May 1993.

From Denver, I made the trip up to Cheyenne WY, not realizing it was a public holiday, when even the UP almost shut down. Just to the west of the town, SD60 6024, SD40-2 3458, 3257 & C36-7 9051 approach with an eastbound manifest freight, and pass SD40-2 3456 & 3733 parked with a train of hoppers.

ATSF SD40-2 5025, 5080 and BN SD40-2 8107 are ready to descend the road from Palmer Lake CO to Denver with a train of coal empties, no doubt returning to one of the coal mines in the Powder River area of Wyoming. June 1993.

I did not expect to have snow in California in June, which then turned to steady rain, but that is what greeted me at Cajon Pass. ATSF SF30C 9524, SD40 5391 and SD45-2 5840 start the descent from the summit with a Twin Stack container working. Note the spray from traffic on Interstate 15!

SP SD45T-2 9393, SD40T-2 8319 & SD45-2 7446 pass Ansel CA with the DOBKU tank train from Dolores yard to Bakersfield.

ATSF B40-8 7420, SD40 5001, SD40-2 5022 & SD45-2 5848 plus two others come down the hill into Mojave CA with an eastbound manifest train.

War bonnets on parade at Tehachapi CA in June 1993. ATSF GP60M 161, B40-8W 543 and three others have reached the summit with an eastbound TOFC intermodal service. TOFC means Trailers on Freight Cars.

CSX GP40-2 6220, B36-7 5850, 5906 and two others are working hard at Savage MD in June 1993. The train is a northbound freight service.

MARC F9PH propels a Baltimore to Washington train out of Savage MD.

Maryland Midland GP9 200 stands at Union Bridge MD in June 1993 with the EnterTrainment tourist set of coaches.

Providence & Worcester Montreal Loco Works built M420W 2005 is on the shed at Worcester MA, but looking somewhat shabby. However, it is an interesting class of loco worth showing. Taken in May 1994.

Three GP40s, 354, 340 & 358 belonging to Guilford Transport Industries (GTI) and all labelled for Boston & Maine, stand ready for their next assignment at Ayer MA.

Standing in a garden above the station at Providence RI, I took this shot of MBTA F40PH-2C 1053 propelling its train out of the station on its return to Boston South station.

The Connecticut Department of Transport had a number of locos used on commuter services around the New York area, painted in the colours of the old New Haven RR initiated by Patrick McGinnis. Here FL9 2024, a class equipped with diesel engine and also third rail electric operation, stands on the extremely sharp curve at Danbury CT in May 1994. The rear of the train can be seen protruding from behind the front of the engine, emphasizing the curve.

There are many services in cities operated by trains which are not loco hauled. In this example, an MNCR class M3 EMU arrives at Brewster NY with a service from Grand Central terminal, New York City.

A view of Croton Harmon station in May 1994, with FL9AC 2043 in the centre with a Poughkeepsie to New York service and an MNCR class M3 EMU waiting on the right.

Amtrak FL9 488 heads the New York to Montral 'Adirondack' past Crugers NY.

Amtrak Gas Turbine units, built under licence from France, sets RTG 158 & 154 emerge from the tunnels at Oscawanna NY in May 1994, working from Schenectady to New York City.

MNCR liveried FL9 2020, and NH liveried FL9 2006 hug the bank of the Hudson River just north of Peekskill NY with a train from New York City to Poughkeepsie.

GATX SD40-2 7363, GTI (B&M) GP40 332, GTI (D&H) SD45 680 leave Binghamton NY with an eastbound manifest freight in May 1994.

SOO line SD60 6006 and SD60M 6058 approach Binghamton NY with a TOFC intermodal service.

Who needs steam trains when you can see this! NYSW C430 3006 switches the yard at Binghamton NY in May 1994, giving the full effect of what happens with an Alco diesel engine when the turbocharger pick up is delayed. Having taken this shot, I then reversed my car and knocked over a fire hydrant, but that's another story!

Nearing the top of a climb near Alburtis PA in June 1994, CR C30-7A 6592, SD50 6823 & GP38 7871 can soon ease off with their eastbound TOFC train.

On the old Pennsylvania main line to the west, CR SD60M 5558, C40-8W 6088 & SD50 6800 head east with a manifest freight near Perdix PA and …

... meet, coming the other way, CR SD60M 5552, SD50 6820 & SD40-2 6412 also working a manifest freight.

GP35 306 of the Allegheny Railroad switches a rake of box cars at the small yard at Johnsonburg PA.

In full sunshine, Buffalo Southern RS11 5010 *Mark Joseph Winter* approaches, long hood forward, with a short freight train at Eden NY.

How about four railroads for the price of one?! The scene is at Tifft Street Bridge, Buffalo NY, one lane being closed so that I could park my car on the bridge. Lucky me! NS GP38AC 2852 & U23B 3914 head a train of auto racks, Allegheny GP40 301 and Buffalo & Pittsburgh GP9 204 switch their sidings, and Mid Louisiana RC MP15 43 & 42 have run round the train of gondolas they have brought up from Lackawanna. June 1994.

Buffalo & Pittsburgh (BPRR) GP40 3100, Rochester & Southern (RSR) GP40 103, Kyle GP40 3111, RSR GP40s 102 & 106, and BPRR GP9 201 bring a manifest freight train towards the Tifft Street yards.

Pinehurst NY sees action on the old NYC water route main line, where CR C40-8 6041, SD40-2 3800, C40-8W 6092 & SD50 6793 head west with a twin stack working. The parallel NS ex Nickel Plate line is shown by the ballast on the right.

SP (SSW) B40-8 8057 and ATSF C30-7 5095 get to grips with the climb out of Benson AZ in October 1995, with a well loaded twin stack container train. On the left in the distance can just be made out the consist of the next train, and visible to the eye, but not the film, was another at the foot of the mountains. Obviously track work had taken place, and in slightly over an hour, seven heavy freight trains thundered past us.

SP SD40-2 8632 & 7313, SD45-T2 9226 and SD40-T2 8341 drag themselves to the summit at Mescal AZ in October 1995, with a mixed twin stack and TOFC train. The old coaling tower, a feature of the picture, was knocked down not long afterwards.

Magma RR GP38-2 3A leaves the mine at San Manuel AZ with a train of ore for the works down the hill.

Magma GP38-2 16 & 18 pass Mammoth AZ with a train of vans from San Manuel to Hayden.

Copper Basin GP9s 203 & 204, with a leased Helm GP number 2027 are stabled with a few ore wagons at Hayden AZ.

At Grand Canyon station, the train to Williams Junction AZ is ready to depart behind FPA4 6773 and GP7 2134. The lead loco was originally owned by the Canadian passenger company VIA railroad.

The classic view at Winona AZ, with the San Francisco Mountains dominating the background, shows ATSF C44-9W 677, SD45 5376 and two others with a priority eastbound twin-stack train of appreciable length and moving fast.

Having taken this shot of ATSF SD40-2 5205, SD45-2 5811, F45 5971 & SDP40F 5262 with a mixed twin stack and TOFC train at Bellemont AZ in October 1995, I was escorted off the bridge by the US Army. I had not realized I was in an Army base!

Rosenberg TX in November 1995 was thrown into chaos by this eastbound manifest freight which managed to block all three road crossings at once whilst carrying out a series of switching moves. With the signal box controlling the flat crossing of the main SP line from San Antonio to Houston with the ATSF line from Fort Worth to Galveston, SP SD40T-2 6866 & 6857, plus SD45T-2 7514 go about causing mayhem.

Passing the signal box at Flatonia TX in pouring rain in November 1995, SP SD40-2 7948, leased EML GP38 764, leased HLCX GP38-2 2602 and SP GP40-2 7946 trundle west with a manifest freight train.

A pair of Galveston Railroad SW 1001 switchers 302 & 304 go about their business in the yards of their home town.

A KCS manifest freight from Shreveport arrives at Beaumont TX headed by SD40M-2 615 & SD60 754, and pass stabled SW1500 4335 & MP15 4367. Taken on a dull November day in 1995.

Rochelle IL is where the UP ex CNW main line from Chicago west to Omaha etc. crosses the BNSF main line from Chicago to Minneapolis and the northwest on the flat. BNSF C44-9Ws 985, 1034 & 1090 in Heritage I livery are working towards Chicago with a twin-stack service in May 1997.

Working west is UP C41-8W 9526, C40-8 9282, SD60M 6327 & C41-8W 9523 with an intermodal service. In those days, with care, you could stand in the middle of the crossing and people let you get on with it. How things have changed!

In colours familiar to British enthusiasts, Wisconsin Central SD45 6511 & 6597 pass the attractively named Honey Creek WI with a southbound manifest freight.

Highlands is a very pleasant small station in the western suburbs of Chicago and here we see Metra F40PHM 192 pulling away from a stop whilst working from Chicago to Aurora IL.

CNW SD40-2 6893, UP SD40-2 3437, GP7 4331 & GP38-2 4600 pass the colourful shrubberies at Elmhurst IL with a westbound manifest train.

Metra Highliner EMU number 220 arrives at the lower level of Randolph Street station, Chicago, in May 1997.

At the slightly higher level at Randolph Street station, three Chicago, South Shore and South Bend EMUs, 1, 16 & 5 wait for custom.

The belt line through La Grange carries a large amount of traffic from several railroads, circumventing Chicago, including Indiana Harbor Belt SD20 2920 running long hood first, hauling a northbound manifest transfer freight. The main BNSF from Chicago west passes over the bridge in the background, adding to the traffic flows.

Viewed from the opposite side of the tracks, NS SD40-2 1631 & C40-9W 9076 are in charge of another manifest train. The power lines seen against the water tower on the right give the effect of a top about to fall over!

The original flat crossing of the UP and BN lines at Grand Island NE was replaced by an over-bridge, on the climb to which BN C30-7 5113, GP50 3151, NS SD40-2 3218, BN B30-7A 4026 & SD40-2 7939 are passing with an intermodal service to Seattle. This makes a change from the endless supply of coal trains to and from the Powder River basin mines. May 1997.

At Aurora NE, an eclectic mix of motive power heads a train of coal empties. In the lead, two BN SD70MACs, 9424 & 9524 are followed by KCS SD60 750, BN C30-7 5580, SD60M 1991 'Desert Storm' & SD40-2s 7186 & 7825.

Fortunately the train stopped further along at Phillips NE, where I was able to walk down the train to take a close-up of 1991, the BN loco painted in honour of the BN employees who had served with the Desert Storm forces in Iraq, showing details for modellers.

CNW SD40-2 6902, with CR C40-8W 7697 and two UP units head west at Gibbon NE with a lengthy train of auto racks in May 1997. This section of the line to North Platte has been progressively widened to accommodate the build-up of traffic on what is the busiest main freight line in the USA.

The view from Daytons Bluff with the city of St Paul MN in the background. Below we see SOO SD60 6047 and CSX C40-8W 7878 passing with a northbound train of tanks, whilst in the Mississippi River a tug boat heads south. May 1997.

BN SD40-2 6700 & 7105 with LMX B39-8 8584 pass St Paul yard with a mixed twin stack and TOFC train heading south.

The rain absolutely buckets down, but I must get a shot of a Dakota, Minnesota and Eastern train. So at Rapid City, SD we see DME SD40-2s 6369 *City of Walnut Grove*, 6055 *City of Chadron* and 6054 *City of Belle Fourche* parked with a lengthy set of hoppers.

I managed to get permission to go round the major BN loco depot at Alliance NE where, amongst other things, was SW1500 27 being serviced.

The Omnitrax workshops in Loveland CO deal with locos of many railroads, but somewhat resident are those of the Great Western Railway. Looking totally unlike those of its British namesake, GP9 211 *Robin* is seen there in May 1997.

Leaving Cheyenne WY in May 1997, a freight train struggles to get moving, not helped by an obviously sick second loco. From left to right the engines are UP SD9043AC 8116, C41-8W 9412, SD40-2 3836 & 3207 and Southwestern RR GP7 2072 DIT (dead in transit).

Starting the climb out of Cheyenne up to the summit of the Rocky Mountains, UP SD60Ms 6289 and 6116 are in charge of a train of tank cars.

The North Carolina Department of Transport sponsored the 'Piedmont' service from Raleigh to Charlotte in the morning and return in the evening. It is seen here on its outward journey at Salisbury NC in October 1997, hauled by special liveried GP40H-2 1768 *City of Charlotte*, the number having historic significance for the state.

One of the pleasures of taking train photos in the USA is that locos belonging to short line groups appear in strange locations. Somewhat away from home territory is Georgia and Alabama RR GP7 2078 posing with a couple of hoppers at Keysville VA.

At their home base in Keysville VA, Virginia Southern RR GP40s 512 & 200 sit in the evening sunshine amongst typical railroad detritus.

NS C40-9 8801 SD60s 6666 & 6556 power their way past Reidsville NC in October 1997, with a southbound coal train.

The northbound Amtrak 'Carolinian' crosses over to the other track in Greensboro NC, hauled by P42-8W 41.

NS C40-9W 9094, GP38-2 5050, B23-7 4005 & C40-9W 9072 leave Greensboro yard NC with a train of TOFC and auto racks from Front Royal to Atlanta, and negotiate the junction to Winston-Salem.

Three CSX trains for the price of one at Hamlet NC in October 1997. From left to right, GP40-2 6439 & slug 2238 on yard pilot duties, in the centre starting to move GP40-2 6152, C40-8W 7766 & GP40-2 6156 with a Philadelphia to Hamlet freight train, and on the right B36-7 5924, 5870 & C40-8W 7768 with an Atlanta to Hamlet manifest freight, waiting its turn.

This was a train that got the locals all excited. SOO SD40-2 772, leased HLCX GP40-2 4000 and CP SD40-2 5955 pass Marston NC on their way from Hoffman to Rocky Mount in October 1997.

The water tower at Mullins SC looks down on Carolina Southern F7As 9163 and 9158 with Waccamaw Coast Line GP18 943, which enjoy the evening sun.

Carolina Piedmont GP10s 8387, 8379 & 8383 pass the time in the small yard at Laurens SC.

CSX B30-7s 5553 & 5530 and SD40-2 8085 accelerate away from Savannah and pass Richmond Hill GA with a southbound manifest freight.

Vidalia GA is the location of the Georgia Central RR offices, where outside were posed GP7 6049 & GP18 3614 with a grain hopper, all for sale. They are in the old colours of this company, not the rather uninspiring current black.

At Cordele GA the NS and CSX main lines from Atlanta to Jacksonville cross on the flat - and does that crossing take a pounding! With the CSX line just visible at the bottom of the picture, NS SD70 2523, GP50 7042 and SP B39-8 8016 appear from behind a southbound freight and pass under a nice signal gantry with a northbound TOFC train.

Georgia Southwestern GP40 1351 & GP38 5124 bracket three cars during a switching move at Cuthbert GA. Seen in October 1997.

The staff very kindly moved Gettysburg RR GP9 105 *County of Adams* out of the shed so that I could take a picture of it. Gettysburg PA in April 1999.

Lancaster Northern GP9 57 tails a short freight train headed by ex TTI U23B 261 heading south from Denver PA.

A pair of CR SD80MACs, 4103 & 4101, are in charge of an eastbound manifest freight near Perdix PA.

In an intermediate colour scheme, Amtrak AEM7 943 stops at Wilmington DE with a New York to Washington NE Corridor service. Note the full height platforms at this rather attractive station. This class was developed from a Swedish design and built under licence in the USA.

Paducah & Louisville RR GP10 8237 & 8604 stand with a train of gondolas at Paducah KY in April 1999.

GP10 1978 was specially decorated by Paducah & Louisville RR to commemorate the Kentucky Wildcats football team's success in 1978. Paducah KY.

Helm Leasing SD40-3s 6507, 6502 & 6506 look very smart at Madisonville KY.

CSX painted a number of locomotives in this orange livery to denote that they were allocated (nominally) for Maintenance of Way duties. At Madisonville KY GP38 9666 stands alongside the loco stabling point in April 1999.

Taking the line avoiding the yards at Madisonville KY, CSX SD50 8552, NS SD60 6588 and CSX GP40-2 6244 head north with a Nashville to Evansville mixed intermodal working.

Two GP16s 1601 & 1603 are about to move down a branch at Guthrie KY to pick up a train of freight cars. The locos are owned by R. J. Corman RR.

Perched on an embankment at Trenton TN, three Alco RSD12s belonging to the West Tennessee RR enjoy the shade in April 1999. In order, the numbers are 1852, 2054 & 1853.

The KWT Railway did me proud by having a manifest freight train actually on the move. GP9 301 is leaving Paris TN in April 1999.

Wisconsin Southern RR painted and numbered SD 20 1848 in commemoration of the establishment of the state of Wisconsin 150 years before. The loco is seen on the loco shed at Janesville WI.

Wisconsin Central, not to be outdone, applied a hand-painted map to the side of GP40 3026. I understand that the work involved meant that it was not allowed to pass through a washing machine, but had to be hand washed! It was moved out for me to photograph at Fond Du Lac WI.

A pair of ex Fox River Valley SD24s 2402 & 2401 (now owned by Wisconsin Central, but still in their original colours) start a transfer freight out of the yards at Fond Du Lac WI.

BN GP40 3503 and BNSF GP39 2931 in an experimental livery speed past the silos at Meriden IL with a train of intermodal flats heading east on the former BN main line from Chicago to Galesburg.

A westbound TOFC passes Flagg Center IL in April 1999 headed by ATSF C40-8W 919, BNSF C44-9W 977 and ATSF C40-8W 810 in respective War Bonnet and Heritage 1 colour schemes.

Priority freight trains are not always handled by the most up-to-date motive power, as can be seen here at Leeds IL in May 1999, where this fully loaded twin-stack train is in the hands of BNSF (still in ATSF colours) GP60 8702, and SD40-2s 6834 & 6801 travelling at full line speed.

The Great Northern built station at Glacier Park MT hosts an eastbound manifest freight, hauled by BN SD40-2 7930, BNSF SD40-2 7095 and ATSF SD40-2 5051. Taken in September 1999.

The classic view of Two Medicine Bridge in Montana sees a pair of BNSF C44-9Ws in Heritage 2 colours bracketing a BN C30-7 hauling a train of grain empties heading east.

Having scrambled up a hillside at Bison MT, a vista opens up showing BN SD60M 9284 and SD40-2 7111 climbing up from the plains towards the summit over the Rocky Mountains with a mixed intermodal train.

Looking the other way from my perch, BNSF C44-9W 4828 & 4759, BN C30-7 5063 and ATSF SD45 5826 head east with a manifest freight, and there aren't many locations that can better this as a scenic railway photo!

Leaving the Rockies behind, an eastbound twin stack with 227 containers (and I counted them all having seen the train earlier and been somewhat impressed) is powered by BNSF C44-9W 4457 & 4353, ATSF C40-8W 843, BN GP50L 3140 & 3125, BNSF SD75M 8271 and BNSF C44-9W 4804 & 4841. Some of these eight locos were DIT (dead in transit) being combined so as to avoid unnecessary track occupancy, but it all adds to an impressive consist.

Montana Rail Link SD45s 375 & 345 and SD45-2 317 head a Missoula to Laurel local service past East Helena MT in September 1999.

The climb west out of Helena MT towards the summit at Mullan Pass requires a high level of motive power to ascend the noticeable incline as seen in this view. Montana Rail Link SD40-2 261, SD45-2 301, ex SP SD45-2 7546 & MRL SD45 388 provide assistance to the main train engines BNSF C44-9W 4905 & 4438.

Whilst inhabiting a tourist office in Butte MT, the sound of a train caught my ear. Without delay, I just caught Rarus GP9 106 & 107 with Montana Western (ex-UP) GP38-2 2010 & 2011 with a westbound freight train in September 1999. Note the capital M letter cut into the top of the volcanic plug.

In the pouring rain common in the Columbia River valley and the Cascade Mountains of Washington state, BNSF C44-9W 4697, 4904 and ATSF C40-8W 859 head a westbound manifest freight past Cook WA in April 2001. I took another photo of this train later on in Vancouver WA and achieved a masterpiece, redolent of steam photos, with a pole projecting out of the chimney. I got a double - one pole from the exhaust outlet and another from the satellite dome!

In Spain, Talgo trains are headed by full-sized locomotives without complicated mergings, so how this abomination was dreamed up escapes me. Amtrak F59PHI 467 approaches Vancouver WA station with a southbound Cascade service from Seattle to Eugene OR.

Gateway Western GP40 3019 and KCS GP40-2L 4702 head east away from Knoche yard, Kansas City MO with a manifest freight train in August 2001, whilst KCS SW1500 switcher 4334 lurks in the corner.

KCS labelled the first of their C44-9W locos with the flags of NAFTA, the North American Free Trade Association. Number 2000 is seen on shed at Knoche yards, Kansas City MO, also carrying the logos of Kansas City Southern RR and its subsidiaries Gateway Western, Texas Mexican, TFM (Mexico) and Panama Canal RR.

Looking very smart with a spark arrestor to show off, Johnson County Airport Commission SW8 1992 sits in the sun at Gardiner KS.

Approaching Topeka KS in the late afternoon an eastbound twin stack stretches the distance behind UP SD70M 4205, SD60M 6326, C41-9W 9444 & C4-9W 9738 which keep the train rolling through the flat countryside.

A general view of the ex ATSF loco shed at Argentine KS, on the western side of Kansas City. A mix of second and third generations of ATSF, BN and BNSF locos are on display in this picture taken in September 2001.

An Amtrak California service from Sacramento, the State Capital, to Oakland (opposite San Francisco) rounds a bend at Pinole, CA in September 2001. The loco is F59PHI 2007. These trains also run services to and from Bakersfield and Oakland along this section of the UP ex SP main line.

The US equivalent of Dawlish in the UK, where the line follows the coast. At Pinole CA, UP SD70M 4405, C41-8W 9322 & 9351 head an eastbound manifest freight along the shore of San Pablo Bay, at the mouth of which is the Golden Gate Bridge. Just behind me is the main BNSF to Richmond, the old ATSF line serving the San Francisco area, so a good place to see trains.

The Altamont Commuter Express company operates trains between San Jose and Stockton CA. In this view, a very smart, clean F40PH-3 3104 is propelling its train of double-deck coaches out of San Jose station.

In an arid part of California, a San Joaquin Valley RR GP9 1754 runs gently along its line with a mixed local freight train near Rio Bravo.

Metrolink is the operator of main line commuter services for the Los Angeles area. In this example F59PH 863 is approaching its destination at Lancaster CA, having left Los Angeles , cut through the San Gabriel Mountains via Soledad Canyon to this town on the edge of the Mojave Desert.

In typical scrub countryside bordering the Mojave Desert, UP C40-9W 9386, 9377 & 9321 head south from Mojave CA towards Lancaster with a manifest freight train.

In a coat of many colours, an eastbound manifest freight exits Tunnel 5 in the Tehachapi CA area with spectacular smoke effects. The locos consist of a GE leading loco and various EMD types following. September 2001.

Showing how dry the countryside has become by September, and how the trains follow the shape of the landscape, BNSF C44-9W 765 & 983 with two other locos head west with a manifest freight and are about to enter Tunnel 2 in the Tehachapi area.

It is nice to have a location named after one's self! At Cable CA, BNSF C44-9W 4784, SD45-2 6508, SD40-2 6798, GP30 2404, GP35 2604 & GP30 2445 snake around the curves below the main road, with a westbound manifest freight in the afternoon of a September day in 2001.

GE C44-9Ws on parade at Tunnel 10 where the line has just completed the famous Tehachapi loop. An eastbound TOFC train is headed by nine BNSF locos in varying shades of the Heritage 2 livery; in order they are 4473, 4567, 4796, 4756, 4544, 4346, 4354, 1098 and 4410 – and didn't I do well to get all the numbers!

Passenger train services between Dallas and Fort Worth TX are worked by Trinity Rail Express. One of their trains headed by F59PH-2 567 is approaching Fort Worth in March 2002, with a four-coach train in its striking colours reflecting the Lone Star emblem.

Leased CEFX SD40-2 3148 and UP SD90MAC 8551 cross the Trinity River Bridge spillway near Fort Worth TX with a southbound manifest freight.

A westbound manifest freight train passes a cotton gin near Start LA in March 2002, behind NS SD40-2s 3384 & 3303 and KCS SD40X 701. The train is heading for Shreveport.

Meridien Southern GP10s 1080 and 1047 carry the colours of the Mid-South RR with appropriate lettering. They go about a spot of switching at their yard in Meridien MS.

When arriving outside the NS loco shed at Meridien MS, my colleague told me not to waste time asking to take photos of their engines, since NS would not allow anyone on their property. However, nothing ventured, nothing gained. So I went to the office where the official answered my request in best English, with the comment 'Stay on the road and don't cross the tracks.' Having taken a couple of ordinary shots for the record, I went to thank him, and he asked whether I had got all the photos I wanted. I replied that there was one interesting engine I couldn't get to, whereupon he said 'Come with me', took me across the lines where I took the shot of South Central Florida Express GP11 9030. So as I say 'Nothing ventured, nothing gained', but the English accent helps!

The station at Meridien MS had been recently refurbished, so to put it on record it is seen with Amtrak P42B-9 84 & 175 stopping with the northbound 'Crescent' from New Orleans to New York City.

Now this was a real stroke of luck, because we arrived at Columbus MS just as Golden Triangle despatched a southbound local service behind GP38-2s 810 & 819. To get it on the move was a real bonus.

The Columbus and Greenville loco shed had a selection of locos in the yard including this one-off GP38 2000 specially decorated to celebrate twenty-five years of service. Seen at Columbus MS.

Another stroke of luck was to find the rare service on the Redmont RR just leaving its terminal at Red Bay AL for Corinth MS in March 2002. The loco is CF7 101 with a single grain hopper; the silos and water tower enhance the picture.

The Tishomingo line was built in conjunction with Tri-State Park MS, a facility to build rocket motors. TISH High hood GP9 222 & 221 keep company with U23B 9553 in the CSX MoW orange colour scheme.

The engineer who designed this bridge obviously got his sums right if what looks like a fairly fragile structure can support a weighty locomotive and train. Leased from Pioneer, GP20 2036 is working a Mississippi Central local freight train near Holly Springs MS in March 2002. This photo illustrates an example of how long freight cars remain in the colours of the original owners, in this case Detroit, Toledo & Ironton which ceased to exist as a separate company in 1983.

GP8 728 & 707 bring a local train of the Arkansas Midland RR alongside a stream near Jones Mills AR.

Once again we strike lucky by coinciding with a train movement on a short line. The Ouachita RR in Arkansas has its operating headquarters at El Dorado in that state, and we arrived just as ex CN GMD1 1159 arrived from Lillie LA making a worthwhile day in March 2002.

At Ashdown AR a KCS manifest freight was travelling south in the morning sunshine behind three SD60s numbers 742, 741 & 732.

The Texas, Oklahoma and Eastern RR was switching its yard at De Queen AR when we arrived to take a photo of GP40 D13 and GP40-2 D16 going about their business.

On the line from Little Rock to Kansas City, westbound coal empties pass Van Buren AR behind UP CW44AC 6597 & 6869 running elephant style.

On the northern side of the summit at Rich Mountain in Arkansas, an empty coal train returning to the Powder River mines in Wyoming was in the charge of a mixed set of locos - KCS C44-9W 2021, BNSF SD70MAC 9933, KCS C44-9W 2037 and BNSF SD70MAC 8959.

At Valiant OK, Kiamichi GP38 3801 and Kyle GP35 2505 were just getting under way with a mixed freight train in March 2002. Two short line locos for the price of one photo!

Leaving Rockville Center station towards Babylon NY, an LIRR M3 class EMU has started its journey in the evening from Penn Station, New York City. March 2002.

At the hub of Long Island railroading, Jamaica, LIRR DE30AC-DM 500 clatters over the track layout with a Long Island City to Port Jefferson double deck commuter service.

You can't see it, but in the distance is New York City. The rain is tipping down at 125th Street Harlem, where P32B-9-DM 210 is arriving with a New York Grand Central to Poughkeepsie train.

A very fortunate sighting of a New York & Atlantic train of mainly wood products occurred at Bellerose, Long Island, where the eastbound service was hauled by GP38-2 261. Note the old Pennsylvania RR style signals on the gantry.

New Jersey Transit electric ALP44 4420 heads a westbound train from Hoboken past Harrison NJ. March 2002.

An Amtrak Acela high speed multiple unit passes Harrison NJ with a Boston to Washington North East Corridor service. What a very uninspiring colour scheme for what ought to be regarded as a premier flagship train.

With the skyscrapers of Newark NJ in the background, Amtrak HHP8 654 heads towards New York City with a semi-fast service, passing Harrison NJ. A neat design of loco, but still a bland colour scheme compared with how Amtrak used to paint their rolling stock.

At Lewiston Junction ME, St Lawrence & Atlantic RR have their main loco shed, on which GP35 3002 and GP40 3004 wait for business in October 2003.

At Concord NH, New England Southern GP10 566 sits in the sun with four loads of cement.

The Amtrak 'Vermonter' leaves the town of its origin, St Albans VT to make its way south to Washington DC behind loco P42B-9 74 with the creeper-covered station building on the right hand side.

One for the modellers. Vermont RR GP40 301 stands in the yard at Burlington VT in October 2003. The loco is named *Rosalie W Szuch*.

A passenger special has stopped at Chester VT with Alco RSI 406 of the Green Mountain Railroad at the head, showing off its well-polished bell.

At East Deerfield MA, a train is being made up by NS C40-9W 9253, ex CR now NS C40-8W 8349 and NS C40-9W 9662. Note that the lead loco carries a full range of warning notices and logos relating to Operation Lifesaver. The yard also hosts locos of Guilford Transport Industries.

Guilford Transport Industries GP9 71 and GP38 252 carry out a switching move at East Deerfield MA. They are on the line leading eventually to Schenectady NY, whilst to the left is the branch line to Springfield.

The Nucor Steel plant at Crawfordsville IN shows off three switchers in different colour schemes. Closest to the camera is 2313, an SW1200 switcher still in colours celebrating the American bi-centennial of 1976; on the right is SW1200 944 in green and yellow, and further away SW1200 1432 in dark blue.

Alco T6 switcher 1017 sits with a train of grain cars at Dana IN in October 2003. The loco is owned by Cargill, the major food and agricultural conglomerate.

What a pretty little engine, and almost perfectly placed. If only one of the coupling rods was perfectly lined up with the other! DTE Energy GE44 Ton No. 1 (did they have a number 2?) is seen at Clinton IN.

The Indiana Railroad provided a special train for the WGRF party, which ran from Indianapolis to Switz City, stopping for photos at various locations, in particular on the very high Tulip Trestle. It is seen here with GP38ACs 31 & 32 and the two-coach train at Holmsburg IN.

Alco RS11 6002 of the Indian Creek RR moves along car by car as the train is loaded with grain at Frankton IN in October 2003.

Specially cleaned and painted for the WGRF group, Respondeks's Tri City Port SW1200 switcher 1206 poses in the sun at Venice IL in October 2004.

Madison yard in East St Louis IL is where the Terminal Railroad Association is in control of all the switching of freight cars. In this view, in the TRRA colours, SD45T-2 3005 with slug 2205 push a trainload over the hump, while SD7R 1751 and slug 2206 wait their turn.

The Manufacturers RR is owned by the Anheuser Busch brewery who uses standard EMD built switchers. But they also own this one-off rebuilt Alco S4 253, which is seen switching grain hoppers at Granite City IL.

Alton & Southern is another St Louis switching railroad, whose locos are painted in the old CNW colours with just different lettering in the logo. Three of their SW1500s, 1517, 1522 & 1508 move a train of grain cars in East St Louis IL in October 2004.

Mittal Steel's Cleveland Works Railway proudly shows off one of its many switchers, this being SW1500 1556 *The Crow* in Cleveland OH. October 2005.

With a plume of exhaust smoke, Ohio Central GP7 1501 gets on the move with a train of steel empties at Conesville OH.

On our way to another location, we found Wheeling and Lake Erie SD40-2 3049 parked by the road, looking clean, so a stop for a photo had to be made. The location was Medina OH.

Bellevue OH is the major hub for NS operations in the north of Ohio, and is very much off limits for the public, even, I was told, for taking photos from the bridge. But my colleagues waited for me to take this shot of NS SD50 5426 and C40-9W 9517 running light alongside the yard hump, with the control tower behind.

Driving along a main road at New Haven OH, the crossing lights started to flash ahead, so a stop was mandatory. And a nice surprise was Ashland RR GP20 2023, SW1500 2467 and GP20 2022 working a local freight train. This was a bonus since we had seen this train earlier, but had been unable to photograph it. Seen in October 2005.

Progress Rail Genset 2002 poses at Aberdeen NC in October 2008. Note the exhaust outlets for the three separate diesel engines. Also note that the white cover over the radiator inlet is not a cover – it is the dome of a building, which I carefully positioned to add to the effect of the loco!

CSX SD70MAC 4525 and CW44AC 19 thunder through Aberdeen NC with a stone train passing the small station building.

South Carolina short line Pee Dee River RR shows off its latest livery on GP16 1797 & 1842, which have a local freight in tow at Tatum SC.

Stabled in the middle of Aberdeen NC are four locos of the Aberdeen, Carolina and Western RR. All four are of Canadian origin, the two in the lead, GP40-2L 9556 & 9552 in the company's own colours, the other two still carrying the livery of Canadian National.

South Carolina Central GP10 77 goes about its business, switching a few cars at Darlington SC. The blueness of the trees is due to the exhaust from what was a not too healthy diesel engine.

The full effect of the latest BNSF colour scheme is seen on ES64AC 6106 & 6146 which have been brought to a stand outside Ravenna NE with one of the lengthy coal trains from the Powder River area. October 2008.

Another of the constant string of coal trains in Nebraska is seen coming over the top of an incline near Sweetwater. The train is headed by BNSF SD70MAC 8890 & 9987 in the Heritage 2 colours.

A storm is approaching from the west and the weather is closing in, but a shaft of sun lights up the scene at Waverley NE where empties returning to the Powder River are headed by BNSF SD70ACe 9152, SD70MAC 9510 & SD70Ace 9278. In the distance, another loco is the tail-end helper of a coal train going east.

A picture that sums up modern railroading in the USA. UP ES44AC 5309 with two others speeds past Odessa NE with a never ending train of twin-stacked containers from the west coast, traversing a deep ballasted, multitrack main line in October 2008.